FAST, STRONG, FEARLESS
FOOTBALL ADJECTIVES

BY MARK WEAKLAND

CAPSTONE PRESS
a capstone imprint

A speedy running back sprints from the backfield, a football clutched in his hands. Around him, grunting linemen push back powerful defenders. **Adjectives** are words that describe nouns. Every person, place, and thing can be described with an adjective. Let's get in the game and use amazing adjectives!

3

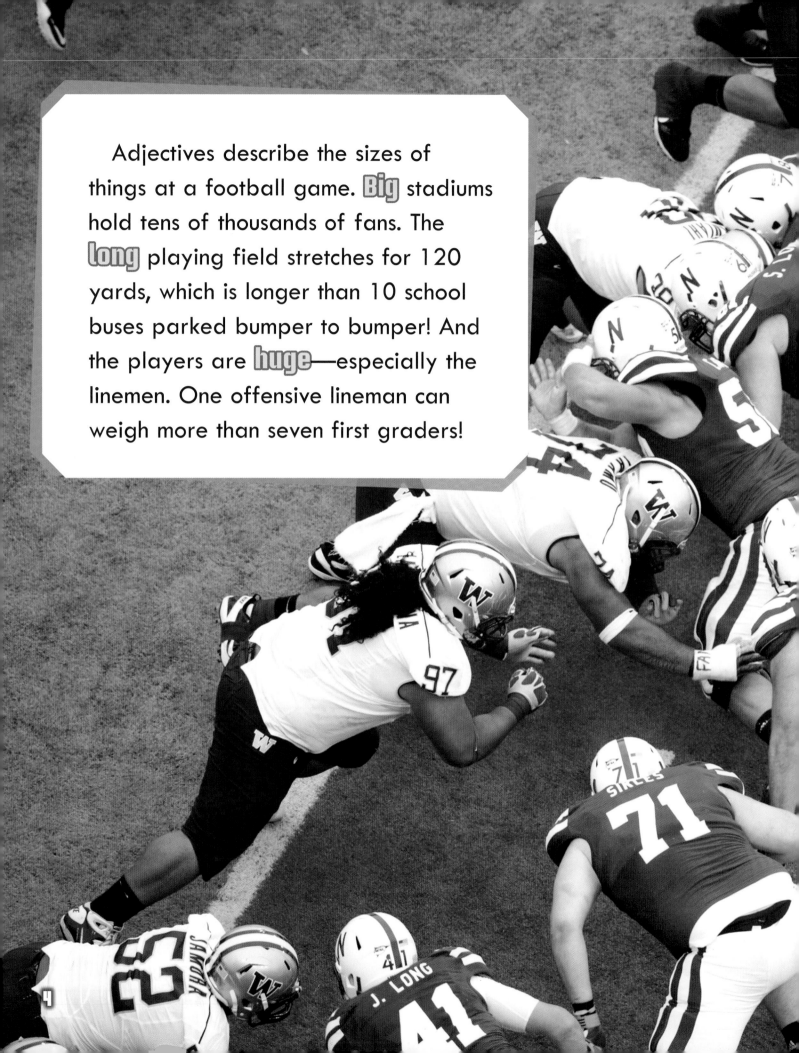

Adjectives describe the sizes of things at a football game. **Big** stadiums hold tens of thousands of fans. The **long** playing field stretches for 120 yards, which is longer than 10 school buses parked bumper to bumper! And the players are **huge**—especially the linemen. One offensive lineman can weigh more than seven first graders!

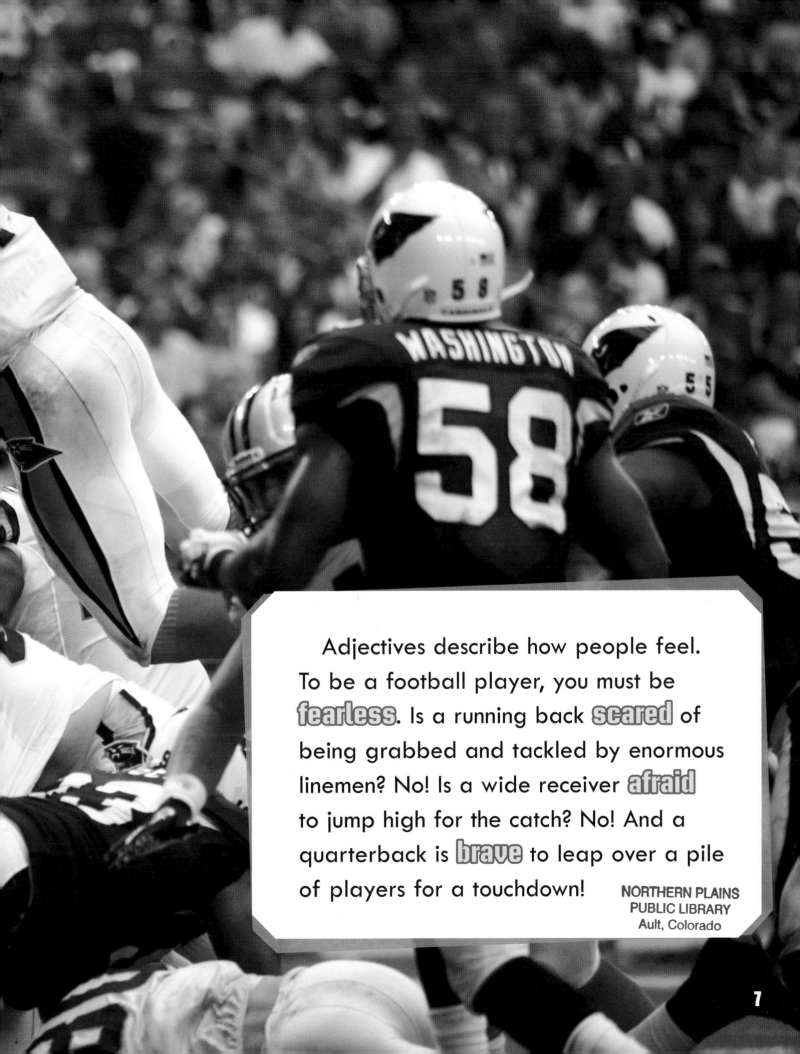

Adjectives describe how people feel. To be a football player, you must be **fearless**. Is a running back **scared** of being grabbed and tackled by enormous linemen? No! Is a wide receiver **afraid** to jump high for the catch? No! And a quarterback is **brave** to leap over a pile of players for a touchdown!

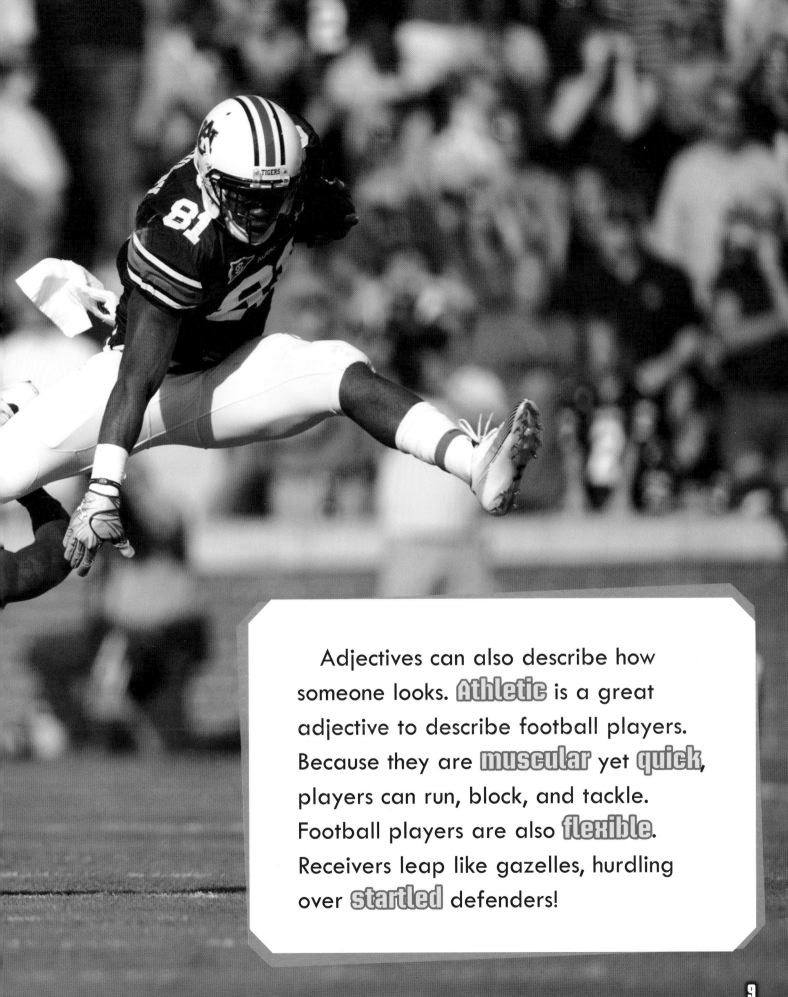

Adjectives can also describe how someone looks. **Athletic** is a great adjective to describe football players. Because they are **muscular** yet **quick**, players can run, block, and tackle. Football players are also **flexible**. Receivers leap like gazelles, hurdling over **startled** defenders!

What adjective describes fans in the stands? **Excited!** When a player scores for the home team, **overjoyed** fans wave their hands and cheer. The **energized** player might even jump into the stands and celebrate with the fans.

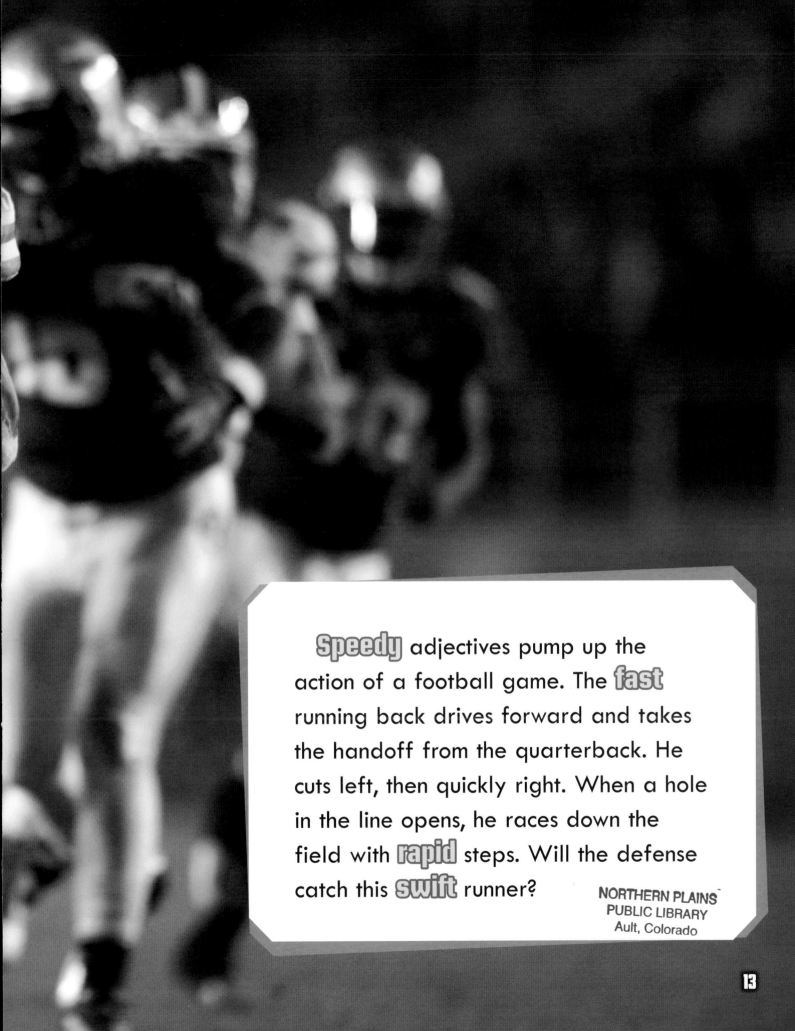

Speedy adjectives pump up the action of a football game. The **fast** running back drives forward and takes the handoff from the quarterback. He cuts left, then quickly right. When a hole in the line opens, he races down the field with **rapid** steps. Will the defense catch this **swift** runner?

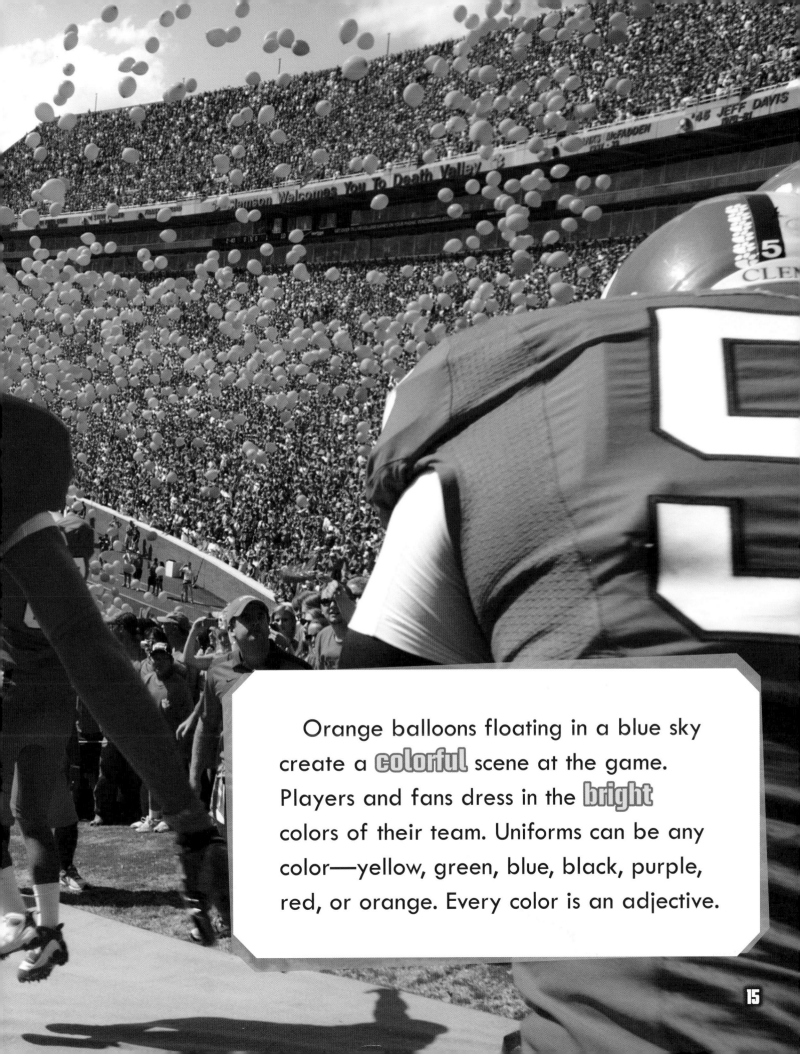

Orange balloons floating in a blue sky create a **colorful** scene at the game. Players and fans dress in the **bright** colors of their team. Uniforms can be any color—yellow, green, blue, black, purple, red, or orange. Every color is an adjective.

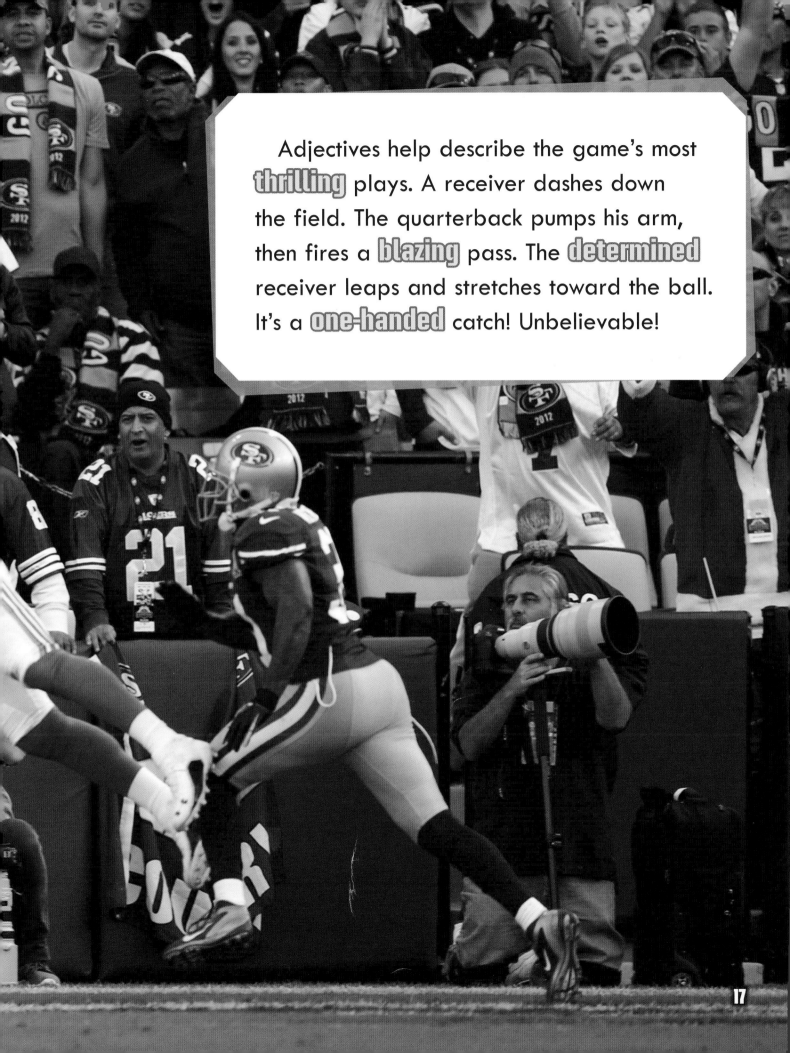

Adjectives help describe the game's most **thrilling** plays. A receiver dashes down the field. The quarterback pumps his arm, then fires a **blazing** pass. The **determined** receiver leaps and stretches toward the ball. It's a **one-handed** catch! Unbelievable!

Football games are often filled with **surprising** adjectives. No one knows what will happen on each play. Just when a team is set to score, a **sneaky** defender leaps to steal the ball. It's an interception! The **unsuspecting** quarterback never saw it coming.

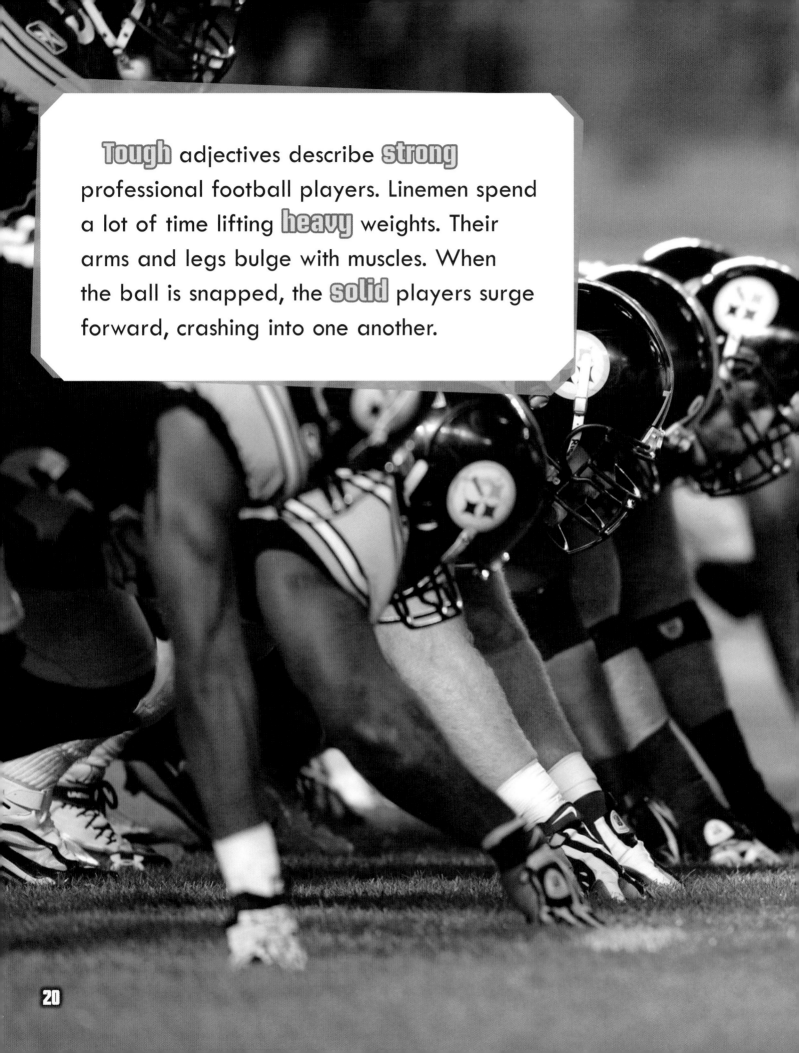

Tough adjectives describe strong professional football players. Linemen spend a lot of time lifting heavy weights. Their arms and legs bulge with muscles. When the ball is snapped, the solid players surge forward, crashing into one another.

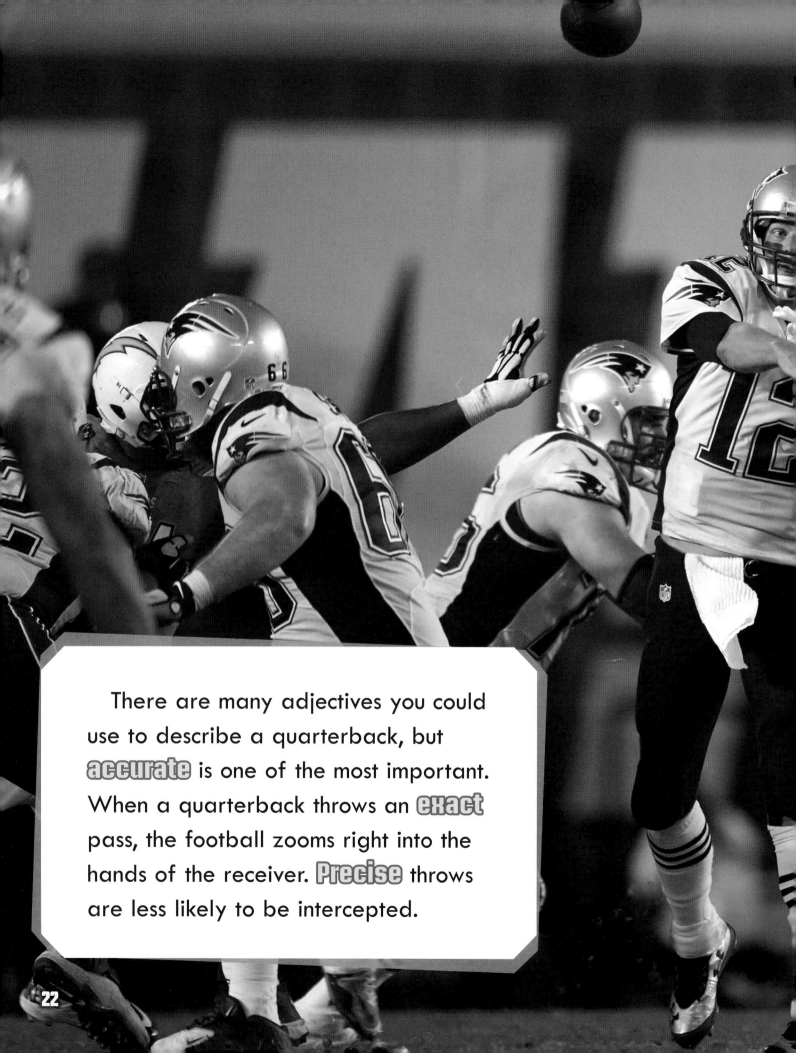

There are many adjectives you could use to describe a quarterback, but **accurate** is one of the most important. When a quarterback throws an **exact** pass, the football zooms right into the hands of the receiver. **Precise** throws are less likely to be intercepted.

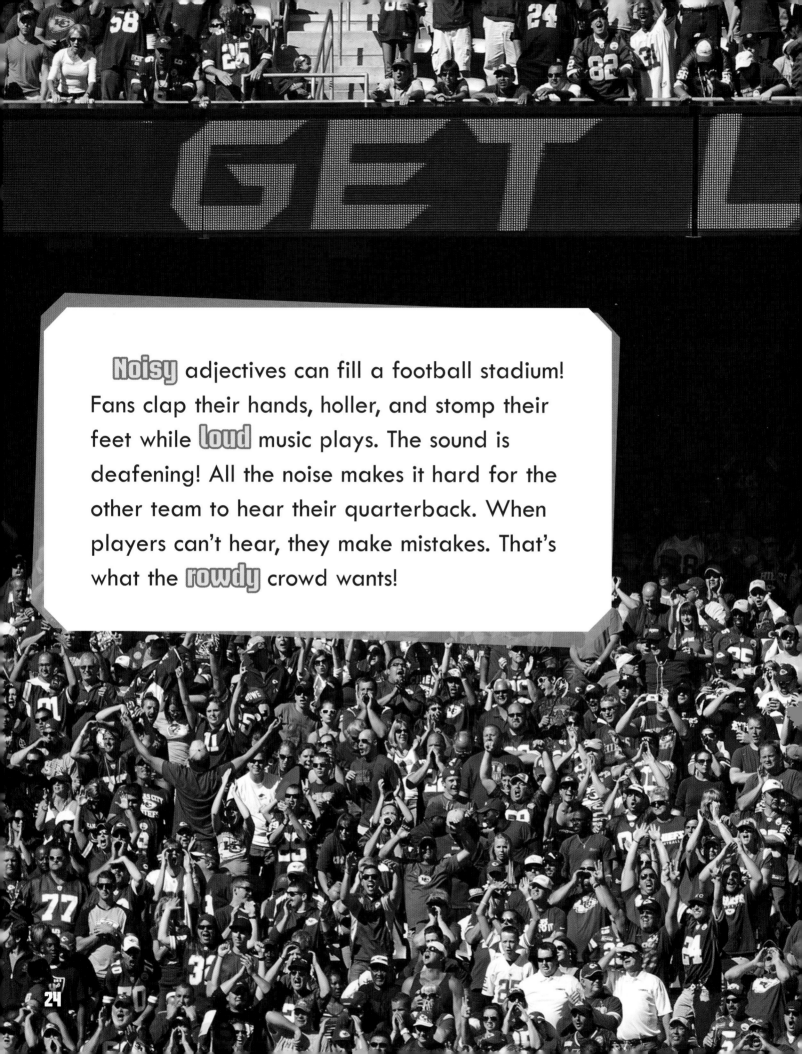

Noisy adjectives can fill a football stadium! Fans clap their hands, holler, and stomp their feet while **loud** music plays. The sound is deafening! All the noise makes it hard for the other team to hear their quarterback. When players can't hear, they make mistakes. That's what the **rowdy** crowd wants!

When a team scores a touchdown, players and fans are **happy**. **Delighted** cheerleaders jump for joy on the sidelines. **Cheerful** fans in the stands wave their arms wildly. In the end zone, **proud** players celebrate with a leap and a shoulder bump.

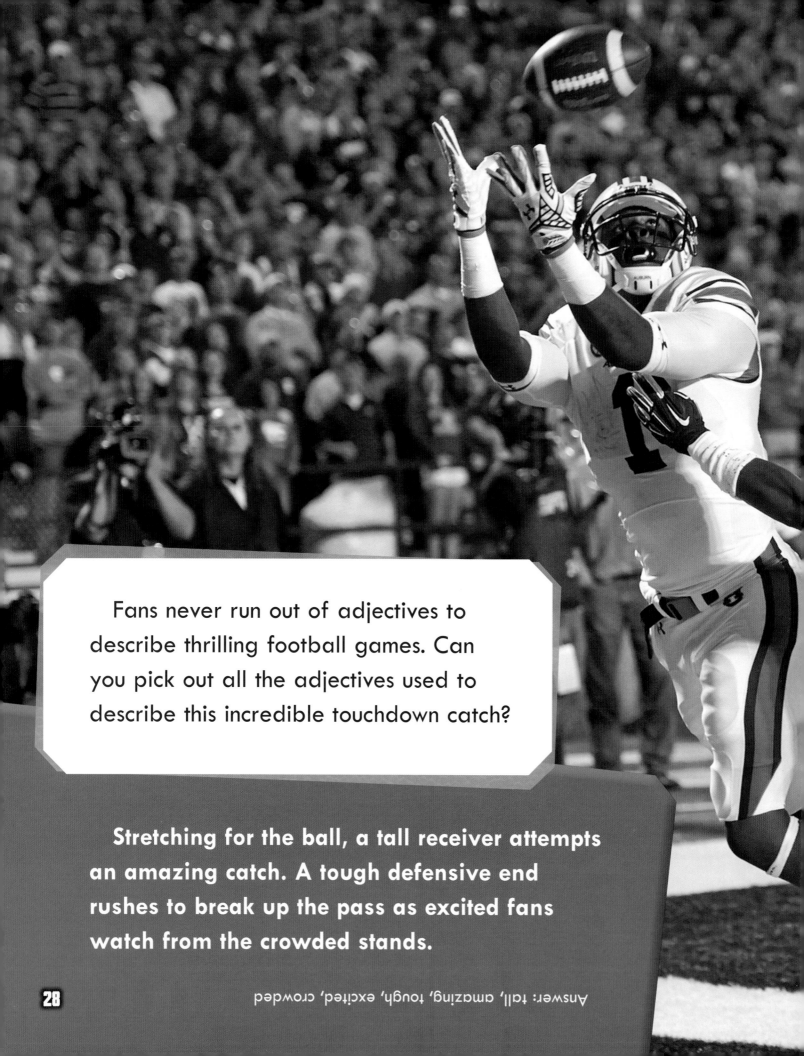

Fans never run out of adjectives to describe thrilling football games. Can you pick out all the adjectives used to describe this incredible touchdown catch?

Stretching for the ball, a tall receiver attempts an amazing catch. A tough defensive end rushes to break up the pass as excited fans watch from the crowded stands.

Answer: tall, amazing, tough, excited, crowded

GLOSSARY

adjective (AJ-ik-tiv)—a word that describes or modifies a noun or pronoun

athletic (ath-LET-ik)—strong and active; having physical skills

colorful (KUHL-ur-full)—having a lot of color

excited (ek-SYE-ted)—having lots of emotion; thrilled

fearless (FIHR-less)—without fear; brave

huge (HYOOJ)—large in size; enormous

noisy (NOI-zee)—full of noise; loud

strong (STRONG)—having physical strength; powerful

surprising (sur-PRY-zing)—causing surprise; unexpected

thrilling (THRILL-ing)—producing strong emotion; exciting

READ MORE

Blaisdell, Bette. *A Hat Full of Adjectives.* Words I Know. North Mankato, Minn.: Capstone Press, 2014.

Cleary, Brian. *Quirky, Jerky, Extra Perky: More About Adjectives.* Words are CATegorical. Minneapolis, Millbrook Press, 2009.

Coffelt, Nancy. *Big, Bigger, Biggest!* New York: Henry Holt and Co., 2009.

INTERNET SITES

FactHound offers a safe, fun way to find Internet sites related to this book. All of the sites on FactHound have been researched by our staff.

Here's all you do:

Visit *www.facthound.com*

Type in this code: 9781620651759

INDEX

Sports Illustrated Kids Football Words are published by Capstone Press,
1710 Roe Crest Drive, North Mankato, Minnesota 56003
www.capstonepub.com

Sports Illustrated Kids is a trademark of Time Inc. Used with permission.

Library of Congress Cataloging-in-Publication Data
Cataloging-in-Publication data is on file with the Library of Congress.
ISBN 978-1-62065-175-9 (library binding)
ISBN 978-1-4914-7602-4 (eBook PDF)

Editorial Credits
Anthony Wacholtz, editor; Terri Poburka and Ted Williams, designers;
Eric Gohl, media researcher; Katy LaVigne, production specialist

Photo Credits
Sports Illustrated: Al Tielemans, 18–19, Bill Frakes, 4–5, 12–13, Bob Rosato, 8–9, David
E. Klutho, 24–25, 28–29, John Biever, 10–11, 20–21, John W. McDonough, 2–3, 6–7,
22–23, 26–27, Peter Read Miller, cover, 1, Robert Beck, 16–17, Simon Bruty, 14–15

Design Elements: Shutterstock

Printed in the United States of America in North Mankato, Minnesota.
032015   008823CGF15